100 WAYS

100 WAYS

Emir Metovic

Illustrated By: **Michael Ascarie**

ISBN: 0692090363
ISBN 13: 9780692090367

In Loving Memory Of

Zejnepe Metovic

1

"Immortal Love"

Immortal love
Find me in the prayer of her wish
Immortal love
Find me from the first touch of her lips
Immortal love
Find me in the depths of her soul
Immortal love
Find me as half a man, but with her, I am whole

2

"My Favorite Kind"

She had a dark mystery
Only for the tortured mind
I must have been mentally ill
Because that was my favorite kind

<u>3</u>

"Loves Only Truth"

There is no value in time, when it is not spent with you
The glass looks half empty, all the scenic places have lost
their view
You wear your heart on your sleeve
And I do too
With all of life's uncertainties
Our love is the only truth

4

"Don't Go"

When we were separated, I lost my every desire
As if your warmth was what fueled me
And your absence put out the fire
Stay with me Darlin, please don't go
You can make it pour rain with the summers heat
You can make the sun shine through winters snow

<u>5</u>

"About Me, About Her"

She wrote about me to ease the pain
Because her thoughts alone she could not trust
I write about her to keep me sane
Because I craved more from just her touch

<u>6</u>

"A Fate Sealed"

My heart is full when I know yours is healed
Let me express the love you desire
For then your fate will be sealed
I'll write you a letter a day for when we are apart
You will be on my mind from morning sun
Until the day turns dark

7

"If I Had To"

If I had to love you through an alley of darkness
Give me this alley with no light, no escape, no harness
If I had to love you in a desert with no air
I will place my lips upon yours
For each breath we can share

<u>8</u>

"Imprints"

Lay your head slowly back
Sounds of the beat melodically dripping slow
I'll lay my imprints all over your body
I'll breathe new life into your soul

9

"Follow Your Heart"

I always follow my heart
And it always leads me to you
If your heart were to skip a beat
Let it skip to the sound you always knew
That sound is the heart beating from my chest
Allow your heart to be entangled with mine
For my heart could not beat on its own
Without yours, it is a straight line

10

"When You"

When you take your next breath
I want to be the air for which you draw in
When you wake in the morning
I want to be the first glimpse you see
When you get dressed to start your day
I want to be each clothing that lies upon your skin
When you seek your one true love
I promise it will be me

<u>11</u>

"I Promise You"

You think no one understands you
Because you are so rare
You're scared another doesn't exist
Like you're the last of its heir
But I promise you I do exist
I promise I am like you
I'll hold my breath waiting until you arrive
Until my face turns blue

<u>12</u>

"How About"

How about I tell her how much I can't stop thinking about her
That I had not stopped to think to take my next breath,
because of how much she has consumed my thoughts
How about I tell her that her substance can be found just
from her smile alone
That the joy she had in simplicity, was the happiness I had
long craved.

13

"Same Beauty"

She thinks I need her doll'ed up, in the fanciest clothes so she can look better
I told her she exudes the same beauty if she were soaked in the rain, head under a newspaper

14

"The Same Meaning"

You look at the moon
I look at the stars
You sing the words
I'll play the guitar
You look for love
I look at you
The meaning is the same
Just a different point of view

15

"My World"

The way her eyes flutter through the words when she
reads a book
The way she makes me fall in love again, with an effortless
look
She possesses a beauty in her soul that only I can see
In a sky full of stars, she is the world to me

<u>16</u>

"The One"

Passion filled her soul, with eyes to match
A mind so mysterious and cruel. One day she made me want to love her
The next, she made me want to detach
It made me covet her more; oddly, for which I cannot fathom why
I was told you receive one in a lifetime
I suppose she was the one in mine

<u>17</u>

"A Souls Desire"

I told her to pour her soul into what she desired
So I could see her eyes light on fire

<u>18</u>

"Her Beauty"

Where did her beauty lie?
In her beating heart
In her soothing soul
In her flickering eyes

<u>19</u>

"Flavor Of Her Love"

The flavor of her love
So good, your tongue would turn numb
For each taste would never be enough

<u>20</u>

"All I've Known"

A scent of her perfume
So familiar, it felt like home
A touch of her lips, onto mine
It's all I've ever known

<u>21</u>

"Your Body"

My lips lay on your stomach
Passing your naval as the lower I go
Your hands run through my hair
As I taste you nice & slow
I can feel your body yearning for it more and more
I won't stop until I have savored everything your body has
to pour

22

"Red Dress"

You in that red dress
Come here
Beauty like yours could end wars
You are a woman of the highest tier
I salivate just looking at you
Wondering if you taste just as good as you appear
If my instincts give me any indication
The answer to such curiosity has become clear

<u>23</u>

"You're My Everything"

You are my dream in a sleepless night
You are my favorite view no matter where the site
I'll love you in the winter; I'll love you in the spring
I'll love you today, tomorrow, and everyday in between

24

"My Queen"

She leaves men shaken
Gasping, just being in her presence
She is a Queen
The world, her throne
And we are her peasants

25

"New Life"

Every time our lips touch, you breathe new life into me.

26

"My Addiction"

As alluring as her name
Her angelic eyes made me take flight
It wasn't just love at first glance
But love with no sight
If I could only have her hand to touch
Her lips to kiss
My satisfaction would be forever cured
My addiction would have its fix

<u>27</u>

"My One Love, My One Life"

You are my poetry
You are the words
You are the pages
You are the thoughts
You are my one love, in this one life

<u>28</u>

"Exploring You"

Her skin smooth, her lips soft
She walks up to me, and whispers, "Lets get lost"
I grab her hand and lead her out the door
No time to get acquainted, just our bodies to explore

29

"In My Heart"

My mind tried to play tricks on me
Tried to tell me things I didn't believe
You were right where I needed you to be
In my heart, setting me free

30

"The Simple Things"

It was the simple things
How she played with her hair
How she laughed when she heard a joke
How she slept after a long day
How she smiled when she looked at me
No material could substitute for that
It was the simple things

31

"Flawless"

Everyone has flaws, or so I thought
Loving her changed my perception
It had taught me a lot
What flaws did she possess?
Were they visible to see?
Love sees no flaws
She was perfect to me

32

"On Your Mind"

They say you think about the one you desire
When the nights become endless
Before the sun starts to beam
I pray I am the one that crosses your mind
Just as your eyes begin to shut
And you fall deep into your dreams

<u>33</u>

"Whatever She Wants"

Her fingers pierced in my back
She's hungry tonight
Her lip prints on my neck
She won't leave without a bite
She tells me to wrap my hand around her throat
She tells me to grab it tight
She is certain in every demand she requests
I assure her she'll receive it just right

34

"Stay With Me"

Tomorrow is not promised
So I'll promise you today
That when you feel lost and don't know where to turn
You'll always have a place in my heart that you can stay

<u>35</u>

"Late Nights With You"

2 in the morning
She looks through the glass window
Rain pouring down, Her book beside her pillow
She circles towards the table, Wine glass all but empty
She turns once more, and says, "What an incredible night"
…As her eyes lay upon mine passionately

<u>36</u>

"Gone Mad"

I have gone mad in your beauty
A devoted urge of wrapping my tongue around your skin
I can take solace in going to hell, Darlin
If your body is the cause for my arrival….for this sin

<u>37</u>

"Lets Get Lost"

Get lost with me
Lets go to a place we've never gone
I'll take you to Nirvana from midnight, till the early dawn
Whatever request, I'll be certain to assist
Satisfying your impulse is the only desire that exists

<u>38</u>

"Lead Me To You"

I was not always wise in my decisions
I have made many mistakes
But if each one lead me to you once again
I would perform those faults a hundred times over
However more it would take

39

"Piece by Piece"

She was broken, in pieces
I asked her if I could mix mine with hers

40

"For You, To You"

Writing for you is a true delight
I never have to force it, it always feels right
If I lose my mind in the darkest of times
I'll find my way back to you
No matter how tall the climb

41

"A Beautiful Thought"

What a beautiful thought
For whenever we are separated
We can look to the sky and be aware
That the moon and the stars give us something at any
moment we can share

42

"One of a Kind"

Many had kindness, many were loyal, many were sweet
But she was different from them all
Qualities no one else could repeat
It might have been unusual to some
To understand my fascination with her
She was crystal clear to me
Every other was a blur

<u>43</u>

"Meant for Me"

If what I find in you is love
Everything else is sprinkles on a cupcake
You wear your heart on your sleeve
For the chances of falling in love eclipses any heartache
This is why I am for you
It is deeper than the sea
It is just as clear as the water
That you were meant for me

44

"Her Slaves"

Brutally scarred, but brave
She has reasons to crumble
But she never caved
Surrender to her at once
Or become one of her prey
She is the Queen of the jungle
And we are her slaves

45

"Nice & Slow"

Smile with your eyes
Fuck, you look good
My hands around your thighs
I wouldn't hold myself back if I could
I'll play a little music
Move your hips with the flow
Anything goes tonight
Lets take it nice and slow

46

"She's My Favorite"

If I were to choose one book to read
She's my favorite
If I were to taste one cup of tea
She's my favorite
If I were to choose one faith for which to leap
She's my favorite
With all the beauty in life that one can receive
She's my favorite

47

"My Intuition"

She loved herself
Her love was secure
For her to love me too
There was nothing more pure
This was true love to me, to receive with no condition
Logic wasn't required
I trusted my intuition

48

"Masterpiece"

God is the greatest artist
His masterpiece was you.

49

"She Is Poetry"

She was a romantic
She was poetry in motion
They assumed a glamour life would charm her
A misconceived notion
She wasn't impressed by outside treasure
She seeked the value of a man's heart as her only measure

<u>50</u>

"Love Letter"

You are a love letter
Written by God
And sent to me

51

"Honey"

Each night
When I put this ink to this sheet
She is my first thought as the ink drips down
Like the first time tasting honey, oh so sweet
If each word has a chance to match her wit
Let the words keep flowing
Until they no longer fit

52

"When You're Ready"

When you are ready to be loved
I will be ready with all of me
If you are not ready to be loved
I will wait until that day, for eternity

<u>53</u>

"Hello"

I remember when my eyes first laid upon yours
My nerves got the best of me
My mind told me to approach you
But my legs didn't agree
My palms began to sweat, I began to over think
Should I say hello? Should I say hi? Should I buy her a drink?
As I finally began to make my way
My mind went blank
The nerves began to overwhelm
My heart began to tank
Then the most beautiful thing happened
Her eyes turned to me, with this magical glow
She said one word, but I knew it would change our lives forever

...She said, "Hello"

<u>54</u>

"Dream Sweet"

Dream sweet, Darlin
When your eyes shut, be where you choose
Because you are a dreamers dream
You are a poet's muse

55

"My Drug"

She was my drug
An addiction I'd gladly accept
A dose of her each day is what kept me alive
Without her, I am simply inept

<u>56</u>

"Fear"

She asked me, "Do you fear love?"
I told her, "I did, until I found the beauty of it, in you.

<u>57</u>

"A Gift"

Every morning I woke up to a gift
A gift of a woman with your love
It could give a man no higher lift
Each moment shared with you
Became better than the last
I've gone mad for you, my sweet
My love grows for you with each gasp

58

"Her Heart"

She walked with confidence
Soulful with each stride
Elegance reigned through her veins
Beauty could not escape her if it tried
What she protected the most
She could never let depart
Her looks may kill
But her greatest asset was her heart

59

"Patience"

Patience my love
All the beautiful things are already here
Why rush looking towards the future
Paint the color each day as it comes
Don't let it smear
We have forever
So lets live in the now
I want to cherish each second with you
For that, I will vow

<u>60</u>

"Sanity"

You are not your thoughts
You are not to blame
When you go a little mad
I'll be here to keep you sane
Let me keep your mind at ease
Let me take away the pain
When you feel like the world is pouring down on you
I will be the sun for which dries away the rain

61

"My Imagination"

I thought a woman like you only existed in imagination
I thought you were make believe
So I touched your hand to make sure you were not just a spirit
To make sure my eyes would not deceive

62

"Lucky Me"

Good does not always come to the good hearted
Bad does not always come to the worst
God gave me you
So I presume I am the luckiest
Because without you
I'd consider myself cursed

<u>63</u>

"My Favorite Book"

You're my favorite book. I read you as slowly as I can. Each word gets further and further from the next so I can enjoy you for that much longer. There is no ending in this book. Just like our love, it is meant for eternity.

64

"I Knew It Was You"

I knew it was you
The way you would laugh watching a comedy
I knew it was you
The way you would mess up the words to the same song
so constantly
I knew it was you
Because each kiss I would give you, felt just as pure as our first
I knew it was you
Because with you, I was at my best
Without you, I was my at worst

<u>65</u>

"Her Taste"

She had this aroma
I did not know which I enjoyed more
Her smell or her taste
The pleasure of having both, no matter the location
Opportunities I'd surely never let go to waste
Tell me how good it is Darlin
What else do you need?
No time to come up for air
Your body is what I fiend

<u>66</u>

"My Peace"

Take me to a place
Where there is no commotion
Where the only sounds I hear
Come from your voice, and the waves of the ocean
Where peace is eternity, where peace is home
If you're there with me, then I will never be alone

67

"Her Eyes"

Her eyes were my everything
My most favorite place to gaze
Whenever I choose to escape reality
I'd get lost in them for days
Once you arrive in the depths of it
You'll never care to go back
A continuing view of any manner without her
Is an aspiration you'll severely lack

<u>68</u>

"Make Room"

If the devil takes you
Tell him to make room for me

<u>69</u>

"My Sweet"

You are my sweetheart
You're sweeter than sweet
Unwrapping and trying all your flavors
You are my favorite treat
Let me have just one taste
For it can never be too soon
Let me scoop that body filled of honey
My mouth will be the spoon

70

"A Silly Thing Called Love"

She was raised in the dark
She felt the pain, the anger
It stuck to her like glue
Then a silly thing called love changed her
It changed to something she wasn't accustomed to

The dark had been pushed out by the light
Love saved her soul
Love gave her reason to fight
Before the dark could swallow her whole

71

"Inch by Inch"

Every inch of you
Yes Darlin, you're blessed and it's a given
Playing hard to get with me won't make me any less driven
Play a little harder
I love the competition
You want your love to be earned
I'm the one to bring it to fruition

72

"What We Believe"

We did not meet in our youth
We may have been older in age
But we didn't know that truth
We went to carnivals
I tried to win you prizes all night long
Sometimes we danced in the middle of the streets
If we didn't have any music
We just sang our own songs
We were young and in love
Or maybe we were just naïve
Others will try to doubt us
All that matters is what we believe

73

"Sophisticated Woman"

What sparkled and shined left little impression on a girl
with your pristine taste
Money could not buy what was valuable and defined for
the love she gave
And for the love she embraced

See, not everyone could keep up
She was stubborn in her ways
She didn't care for the criticism
She didn't care for the praise

<u>74</u>

"Worth The Wait"

I've waited for you all my life
And it was well worth the wait
I never believed in meant to be
But now I see you were truly my fate
What you have given me is more than just love
More that just bliss
You made me feel elevated amongst the clouds
After finding me sunken deep into a dark abyss

<u>75</u>

"Just To See You Smile"

I can't help but love the way you smile
It's like seeing the sun come out and stop the rain
You say loving you is like walking a thousand miles
Then I will run to you
Let it be in quicksand, or in chains

<u>76</u>

"A Tough Flower"

She is a flower
Just as she grew and found solace from all the hurt
She grew and became a flower through the cracks of the
cements dirt
Limits should not be placed on what she can do
Her drive and her strength will conquer any hurdle you
try to put her through

77

"Falling In Love With You"

She loved bookstores
It made her feel at home
The genre was not of importance
She read anything that let her mind roam
I would sit and just watch her read
The way the pages made her eager as her eyes stretched open with each turn
I knew right then and there
That she was the only woman who can make me eternally yearn

78

"Forever With Her"

She placed her hand upon her cheek
Gazed at the stars, she could have gazed for a week
She loved nature, for nature used no words to speak
It spoke in the beauty seen through her eyes
Eyes that could make a strong man weak
She is the star, the nature, and the eyes for which makes
her unique
Through her lenses, you can see the world's obvious
treasures and its hidden mystique
I want to live in her eyes forever
Because it has all for which I wish to seek
I wished for love
And I have reached it in her, at its peak

79

"Dangerous To Love"

She was dangerous to love
Self destructive in her ways
It was like trying to change a raven to a dove
Luckily, I did not try to change her
But to be the medicine for which she was void of
If the art was in the danger of loving her
Then that danger fit me like a glove

<u>80</u>

"Her Lips"

Her lips pressed on the glass
The marks of her lips leave a print
If only I could be that glass
To touch those lips and taste her sip

<u>81</u>

"What Will You Say?"

She asked me
What will you say?
When the birds no longer sing, when the trains fall off the tracks
What will you say?
When what tied us together broke its string
What we thought was so perfect, had its cracks

I will say

That loving you conquers any challenge that life may bring
That love is the cure of any beauty in life that may lack

<u>82</u>

"A Life Without You"

If I have survived all these years up until I have met you
Then I know there's nothing that I cannot endure
Because once a day with you has been spent
A life without your company, has lot its allure

83

"To Be In Love"

To love, and to be in love are not in all the same
To love makes you feel the warmth
To be in love, you become the flame
With her, I was immersed in both
Something so picture perfect, there wasn't use for a frame
Her love was my most coveted honor
Her love was the strongest acclaim

<u>84</u>

"My Destination"

If happiness was a place
And not a state of mind
It would not be difficult to trace
It would be easy to find
A map wouldn't suffice, nor would its duration
My happiness is placed with you
You're the destination

<u>85</u>

"My Guilty Pleasure"

It's my guilty pleasure
To see you get dressed for the evening
It's my guilty pleasure
To bite your lips when you're close and your eyes give me
a stare
It's my guilty pleasure
To grab all of you in that tight dress as you're leaning
It's my guilty pleasure
To tell you that you're pleasure is the only one I crave
For no one else can compare

<u>86</u>

"Each Day"

Each day
As I love you more and more
I sit still and am left to turn back the clock
To the days I had nothing
Then out of the blue, your love rendered me speechless;
your love began to talk
You said, "That when you feel out of sorts, and when you
feel you have lost your way

Close your eyes and count to three

Walk to the sound of my voice,
that's where my love will be."

<u>87</u>

"Your Strength"

Show me what you believe is your greatest flaw
I will show you it is in fact your greatest strength

<u>88</u>

"Each Moment"

Walking barefoot in the sand
Your fingers in-between mine
Your skin lay beneath the sun as it begins to tan
You tell me you have butterflies in your stomach
I have chills down my spine
As our feet hit the water
You tilt your head on my shoulder as we watch the waves
topple through
This moment felt too good to be real
Each moment with you is too good to be true

<u>89</u>

"Love Makes You"

Love makes you
See when your eyes lay to rest
Love makes you
Fly when you are left without wings
Love makes you
Feel your heart pound outside your chest
Because love makes your heart want to jump out and sing
Love is the most simple
Love is the most pure
Love is the answer to every prayer
Love is the cure

<u>90</u>

"A Brush Of Our Love"

Use this brush and paint me a picture
Paint me your deepest desires
Paint me your deepest fears
Use this to erase what has expired
Paint the future you seek as it nears
Halfway through, she stopped, and handed me the brush
A puzzled look lay across my face, she then began to blush

I asked, "My sweet, how can I know what your future may
hold?"

She smiled and said,
"My future rests with yours
Without you, my story cannot be told"

91

"My First & Only"

I waited for someone like her, for what seems like a lifetime.
I had doubts it would ever happen.
But once I saw her, I knew.
She was put on this earth for me. I was put on this earth for her.
She was my first love. She was my only love.

92

"My Hands"

My hands
Attached to her body, as if they were sewed as one
Her skin, like a magnet
Not to obey, and I'd rightfully be shunned
She said she was mine, from her head down to her feet
I didn't know where to begin
For every part of her body was a fulfilling place to greet

<u>93</u>

"You Deserve"

You deserve
Good company when it's late
You deserve
A long kiss on those soft lips
You deserve
A romantic drive through the golden gate
You deserve
Arms to catch you incase you slip
You deserve
A shoulder to cry on when you're weak
You deserve
A painting of your beauty and all that it beholds
You deserve
Someone who gives you love at loves highest peak
You deserve
True love forever, no matter how life unfolds

<u>94</u>

"Crystal Clear"

She had soul
You can see it through her heart
You can see it in her eyes
If her affinity for you was strong
She would protect you deep into the ocean
She would protect you high into the sky
Being loved by such a woman
Would be any mans greatest honor that can be achieved
Attain such prestige at its highest of value
To seek anything more is a waste to conceive

95

"I Adore You"

Oh how I adore you, Darlin
Who is better at loving me, than you?
Who can bring joy, just from the sound of your voice?
I wouldn't have a clue
No one can make me forget my troubles so easily
That's why I love you like I do
When I need you the most
Without saying a word, you always know your cue

96

"Floating In Your Love"

She defies gravity
I feel like I am floating in air
This must be a dream
If so, please don't make me aware
I don't know how long this feeling will last
Your guess is as good as mine
I hope it's until my final breath
If so, I'll be just fine

97

"Maybe It's Love"

Maybe it's love.
I cant put my fingers on it. There's something positively
unique about her
Someone may say the same words, or do the same things
and she does, but it comes out uniquely from her. It's
completely different.
Whenever she does something, no matter how ordinary
most people would label it, it's the opposite to me.
It's extraordinary. It's beautiful and distinct.
Only she can do it. Only she can have this affect on me.
No one else.
Maybe it's love.

<u>98</u>

"Take Me There"

I told her, "Close your eyes"

I placed my fingers over them to be sure

I told her, "Think of a place you most want to be
A place that brought you a calm, a happiness that was pure"

I felt my fingers begin to move up slightly
From the smile forming on her face
She grabs my hands to her lips
Then down to her heart they are placed

She turns to me and says,

"Why close my eyes and try to imagine something I
already knew?
My most happiest place on this earth is every place that is
with you"

99

"Reborn"

Try to tear down her wall
She'll build another with her bare hands
You can't break her when what has broken her, she restored
Your attempt will fall flat, her strength too strong to withstand

She is reborn

Her is heart full, after countless aches
I promised to love her, for her courage and for her soul
A promise I vowed never to break

<u>100</u>

"Serenity"

She is serenity in motion
She is the wave, she is the ocean
She is the peak at the top of the mountain
When I thirst for her, she is my fountain

AUTHOR'S NOTE

I was raised in the Bay Area but am originally from Bar, Montenegro. I have enjoyed writing for a long time, but never thought to write a book. My passion has encouraged me to follow through and do so. I encourage you not to read this book all at once, but little by little. I believe poetry should be read when you want to feel something, when you desire for words to be powerful enough to move you. To move you when you want to relate to something. When you want to connect and reestablish passion with yourself and with love. If my writing moves you, even for just one out of the 100 that I have written, then I can feel assured writing this book was well worth it.

www.ingramcontent.com/pod-product-compliance
Lightning Source LLC
Chambersburg PA
CBHW021934040426
42448CB00008B/1069